TrueU: Does God Exist?

Copyright © 2012 Focus on the Family. A production of Focus on the Family. All rights reserved. International copyright secured.

A Focus on the Family book published by Tyndale House Publishers, Inc., Carol Stream, Illinois 60188

Focus on the Family and the accompanying logo and design are federally registered trademarks of Focus on the Family, Colorado Springs, CO 80995.

TrueU is a trademark of Focus on the Family.

TYNDALE and Tyndale's quill logo are registered trademarks of Tyndale House Publishers, Inc.

Cartoons by Ed Koehler

Editor: Ray Seldomridge

Cover design by Al Navata

Cover background elements copyright © by iStockphoto. All rights reserved.

ISBN: 978-1-58997-691-7

Printed in the United States of America

17 16 15 14 13 12 11
7   6   5   4   3   2   1

DOES
GOD
EXIST?

building the scientific case

01

EW

Can we absolutely prove the existence of God, or are we left to grapple in the dark and take blind leaps in order to believe? Is there a third approach to faith that provides a better way?

In this introductory lesson, Dr. Meyer discusses the nature of biblical faith and shows how we can use science and logic to examine the great questions of life. By looking at the evidence all around us, we will build a case for the existence of God.

QUOTE UNQUOTE

What did Dr. Meyer say? Fill in the blanks as you watch his presentation..

1. Students are annoyed to be told that they ought to believe the Bible because _____ _____ says so.

2. Do you ever run into the idea that _____ is what you believe in but you're not really sure is going to happen?

3. Faith might be something you believe in for which you have some really good _____.

4. Scientists have faith that the _____ they make from evidence are actually true.

5. Sometimes faith is a kind of _____ thing: "I have faith that God is with me. I have faith in God's presence or power."

6. I want us to be _____ on the kind of faith that we're going to be providing reasons for.

7. Faith is also belief in a system of thought or a personal philosophy—a _____.

8. The most important question a worldview answers is, What is the _____ _____?

9. Nobody gets absolute _____ of anything.

10. We're going to look at _____ from the natural world and see which one of these big worldviews provides the best explanation of that _____.

WHAT'S REALLY REAL?

Every attempt to explain the universe is based on one of four different, conflicting worldviews— materialism, pantheism, deism, and theism.

BEYOND MERE HOPE

Our "faith" in the theistic—specifically biblical—worldview is not a baseless, subjective hope or wish but rather a confident, thoughtful embrace of that interpretation of reality.

A REASONABLE CONCLUSION

Our belief in theism (a personal God) is based on reason— on evidence in the natural world that is best explained by this worldview rather than another.

PROFESSOR SAYS, YOU SAY

Discuss as a group what you would say if your teacher or professor asked the following question in class:

ISN'T THE *REAL* REASON YOU BELIEVE IN CHRISTIANITY SIMPLY THAT YOU WERE RAISED IN A CHRISTIAN HOME, OR THAT YOU WISH LIFE HAD MORE MEANING THAN IT DOES?

You can refer to your notes, if you took any during Dr. Meyer's lecture. Support or add to one another's responses, bringing in any relevant Bible passages. Perhaps you'd like to role-play the dialogue, taking turns to represent the skeptical professor.

WHAT OTHERS SAID

"Physicists have placed their faith in the idea that deep down the universe is coordinated by a great plan, a rational system of organization, a hidden but accessible scheme, one that when finally seen in all its limpid but austere elegance, will flood the soul with gratitude."

—David Berlinski

"Faith is a living, bold trust in God's grace, so certain of God's favor that it would risk death a thousand times trusting in it."

—Martin Luther

"All these people were still living by faith when they died. They did not receive the things promised; they only saw them and welcomed them from a distance. And they admitted that they were aliens and strangers on earth. People who say such things show that they are looking for a country of their own."

—Hebrews 11:13-14, NIV

WHAT IS WHAT? *A matching quiz*

Draw a line from each term in the first column to its definition in the second column.

1.	**PRESUPPOSITION**	A. a suggested (but not explicit) meaning
2.	**CONNOTATION**	B. reasoning from effects back to a cause
3.	**INFERENCE**	C. hypothesis about ultimate reality
4.	**WORLDVIEW**	D. to generalize from observation
5.	**PRIME REALITY**	E. conclusion based on evidence or reason
6.	**THEISM**	F. thing from which everything else comes
7.	**DEISM**	G. God made the world but does not intervene in it
8.	**PANTHEISM**	H. something you assume to be true
9.	**DEDUCTION**	I. the forces and "stuff" of nature are god
10.	**INDUCTION**	J. applying a general rule to a particular case
11.	**ABDUCTION**	K. a personal God created the world and acts in it

LESSON 2

THE BIG BANG COSMOLOGY

— THE FINITE UNIVERSE

Edwin Hubble discovered evidence for the "Big Bang" while peering through the Hooker telescope on Mt. Wilson in California.

02 OVERV

Has the universe always been here, or did it have a beginning? Why should we care? In this lesson, Dr. Meyer traces the growth of scientific materialism and how it not only conflicts with the Bible and the founders of science, but also fails to account for some exciting, recent developments, particularly the discovery that the universe is expanding from a finite point in time and space.

Richard Dawkins and the other "New Atheists," as well as many scientists who want to believe in a world without God, are feeling threatened today. For they know that if the world had a beginning, some force or being outside the universe would have had to provide the cause.

EW

QUOTE UNQUOTE

What did Dr. Meyer say? Fill in the blanks as you watch his presentation.

1. The physical world, according to St. Paul, is revealing something about the reality and attributes of the _____.

2. The _____-only lobby is very strong, and most textbooks include only a discussion of his theory and no evidence against it.

3. The early founders of science not only made advances in their scientific disciplines—physics, chemistry, etc.—but they also made _____ arguments.

4. How did we get from Newton, saying that the evidence of the physical world reveals the handiwork of the Creator, to _____ , who says just the opposite?

5. At the time, physicists believed that the universe was _____ in time and space.

6. In the theistic worldview, it's _____ first, matter second.

7. In the materialistic worldview, it's_____ first, and _____ has been there from eternity past.

8. Actually, the New Atheism is the old _____ repackaged to make bestsellers.

9. Hubble discovered that the farther the galaxy was away, the _____ it was receding.

10. If you have an expanding universe, what happens if you go back in time? You've got a _____ _____.

11. If there's a beginning, there must be something to _____ the beginning—something that isn't the universe itself.

12. Obviously there's something about the discovery of the finite universe that's _____ to a lot of physicists and astronomers.

WHAT'S THE BIG IDEA?

ST. PAUL AND THE SCIENTISTS

Belief in a personal, rational God was held not only by the ancient writers of Scripture, but also by the founders of modern science in the 16th and 17th centuries.

SCIENCE LOSES ITS WAY

The 19th century saw a dramatic move away from theism toward undirected evolution (materialism) in all the scientific disciplines.

THE UNIVERSE TALKS BACK

Recent discoveries in physics and astronomy have undercut the idea of an eternal, self-existent world and instead support the biblical claim that the universe had a beginning.

PROFESSOR SAYS, YOU SAY

Discuss as a group what you would say if a college professor asked this question in class:

WHAT POSSIBLE REASONS COULD YOU HAVE FOR QUESTIONING THE ESTABLISHED FACT THAT LIFE BEGAN ON ITS OWN AND EVOLVED NATURALLY OVER TIME?

You can refer to your notes, if you took any during Dr. Meyer's lecture. Support or add to one another's responses, bringing in any relevant Bible passages. Perhaps you'd like to role-play the dialogue, taking turns to represent the professor.

WHAT OTHERS SAID

"It is absolutely safe to say that if you meet somebody who claims not to believe in evolution, that person is ignorant, stupid or insane." —Richard Dawkins

"I had the intention of becoming a theologian ... but now I see how God is, by my endeavors, also glorified in astronomy, for 'the heavens declare the glory of God.' " —Johannes Kepler, 1571-1630

"I study the book of nature, and ... I find myself oftentimes reduced to exclaim with the Psalmist, 'How manifold are thy works. O Lord! in wisdom has Thou made them all!' " —Robert Boyle, 1627-1691

"The Big Bang was not an event taking place at a time or in a place. Space and time were themselves created by the Big Bang, the measure along with the measured." —David Berlinski

WHAT IS WHAT? *A matching quiz*

Draw a line from each term in the first column to its definition in the second column.

1. **NEW ATHEISM**

    A. the science of the origin and development of the universe

2. **INTELLIGIBLE**

    B. discoverer of the universe's expansion

3. **GOD HYPOTHESIS**

    C. recent group of authors who call themselves anti-theists

4. **COSMOLOGY**

    D. having a limited existence; not always here

5. **FINITE**

    E. Einstein's fudge factor for a static universe

6. **MATERIALISM**

    F. understandable; product of a rational mind

7. **HUBBLE**

    G. matter and energy are everything and have existed forever

8. **BIG BANG**

    H. the universe was designed by God

9. **REDSHIFT**

    I. the universe's beginning (it has not always existed)

10. **COSMOLOGICAL CONSTANT**

    J. effect on wavelength of receding objects

LESSON 3

THE BIG BANG COSMOLOGY

— IN THE BEGINNING

Using the Holmdel horn antenna at Bell Telephone Labs in New Jersey, Arno Penzias and Robert Wilson in 1965 discovered the background radiation that confirmed the Big Bang theory and the expanding universe.

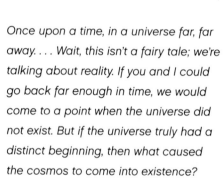
© NASA

Once upon a time, in a universe far, far away. . . . Wait, this isn't a fairy tale; we're talking about reality. If you and I could go back far enough in time, we would come to a point when the universe did not exist. But if the universe truly had a distinct beginning, then what caused the cosmos to come into existence?

According to Dr. Meyer, the Big Bang theory best describes the dawn of the universe. But the Big Bang (or "first effect") requires a "first cause." So what caused the Big Bang? Dr. Meyer contends that, based on the evidence, theism has the most convincing answer. Naturalism and pantheism both fail to provide a cause that could bring the cosmos into existence.

QUOTE UNQUOTE

What did Dr. Meyer say? Fill in the blanks as you watch his presentation.

1. Fred Hoyle thought that the universe should maintain a steady, constant _____.

2. If you've got two theories that explain the same piece of evidence equally well, you look for _____ evidence.

3. According to the oscillating universe idea, ... eventually the gravitational force produced by all the matter in the universe is going to cause a _____.

4. The measurements show that there's only a small fraction of the _____ you would need in order to cause a gravitational recollapse.

5. The universe is not only expanding outward, but it is _____ in its rate of expansion.

6. Stephen Hawking was able to solve what are called the _____ _____ of general relativity.

7. As you go back in time, the curvature of space gets infinitely _____.

8. According to Hawking's solution, not only is there a zero point in time, but there's a zero point in _____ as well.

9. A number of Christians object to the _____ _____ as if the physicists were saying it caused the universe to come into existence. But the _____ _____ doesn't tell you what caused that first event.

10. If you're talking about the origin of space and time itself, then you need something that exists _____ of space and time.

WHAT'S THE BIG IDEA?

NOT A BANG BUT A WHIMPER?

Scientists who dislike the idea of a definite beginning to the universe (the "Big Bang") have suggested other theories to get around it.

THE UNIVERSE HAS ALWAYS BEEN HERE!

WHY? HOW?

JUST BECAUSE, THAT'S WHY. DON'T ASK QUESTIONS!

ECHOES OF GENESIS

The "field equations of general relativity" prove that the universe began at a zero point in both time and space, which coincides with the biblical doctrine of creation out of nothing.

SOMEONE TO GET IT STARTED

Theism, but not pantheism or materialism, has the causal power to produce the evidence we see of a finite universe.

PROFESSOR SAYS, YOU SAY

Discuss as a group what you would say if a college professor asked this question in class:

OKAY, OKAY, SO IT SEEMS THAT THE UNIVERSE HAD A BEGINNING AFTER ALL. BUT AREN'T YOU READING TOO MUCH INTO IT TO TAKE IT AS EVIDENCE FOR YOUR BIBLICAL VIEW OF CREATION?

You can refer to your notes, if you took any during Dr. Meyer's lecture. Support or add to one another's responses, bringing in any relevant Bible passages. Perhaps you'd like to role-play the dialogue, taking turns to represent the professor.

WHAT OTHERS SAID

Universe with a Plan

"There is a coherent plan in the universe, though I don't know what it's a plan for." —Fred Hoyle, who made up the term "Big Bang" to mock the idea that the universe had a beginning

"Astronomy leads us to a unique event, a universe which was created out of nothing, one with the very delicate balance needed to provide exactly the conditions required to permit life, and one which has an underlying (one might say 'supernatural') plan." —Arno Penzias, co-discoverer of the background radiation that confirmed the Big Bang theory

WHAT IS WHAT? *A matching quiz*

Draw a line from each term in the first column to its definition in the second column.

1. **HOYLE**

2. **CONTINUOUS CREATION MODEL**

3. **STEADY STATE THEORY**

4. **GAMOW**

5. **BACKGROUND RADIATION**

6. **OSCILLATING UNIVERSE**

7. **CREATIO EX NIHILO**

8. **SINGULARITY**

9. **LAWS OF NATURE**

10. **INFLATIONARY COSMOLOGY**

A. 2.7 degrees above absolute zero

B. another name for the steady state theory

C. universe has always been expanding, always adding matter

D. descriptions of how material parts of the universe interact

E. creation out of nothing physical

F. universe is like an accordion

G. exponential expansion of the universe shortly after it began

H. architect of the steady state theory

I. scientist who calculated remnant energy from the Big Bang

J. point where space and time didn't exist

LESSON 4

THE BIG BANG COSMOLOGY
— A FINELY TUNED UNIVERSE

04 OVERV

In this lesson, Dr. Meyer introduces the "anthropic fine-tuning principle," highlighting evidence that the universe runs according to specific, intelligent laws of physics and cosmology that allow life to exist. If the universe looks finely tuned for life, then maybe there was a Fine Tuner, someone who set up those life-sustaining parameters.

The materialistic worldview has significant problems with this theory, so who is right? Is it mere chance that life came into existence? Was life simply necessary? Or does the fine-tuning principle demand an intelligent source acting outside the space-time universe? Let's allow the evidence to suggest some answers.

QUOTE UNQUOTE

What did Dr. Meyer say? Fill in the blanks as you watch his presentation.

1. There is compelling evidence for the _____ design of the entire universe.

2. The universe is expanding at a very precisely calibrated rate. If it were going even a tiny bit _____, there would be no structure in the universe—no galaxies, no planets.

3. If that expansion rate were even a little tiny bit smaller, the gravitational force produced by matter would cause the universe to _____ back onto itself.

4. Everything seems to be _____ _____. We live in the _____ _____ universe.

5. Later in his career, Fred Hoyle started to sound strangely _____.

6. It looks like the universe was a _____ _____.

7. _____ alone does not trigger awareness of design.

8. What triggers design is when you've got a really improbable event which also conforms to an independently given _____.

9. The weak anthropic principle confuses a necessary condition with a _____.

10. We tend to prefer explanations that aren't super _____.

OUR JUST-RIGHT UNIVERSE

The universe is fine-tuned to make life possible on earth. The slightest variation in certain physical constants would make life nonviable.

The forecast calls for 1,000° today.

I'll be glad when summer is over!

THE MIND BEHIND THE MATTER

This fine-tuning of the laws of physics and chemistry provides compelling evidence for the intelligent design of the entire universe.

A WEAK ARGUMENT AND A COSMIC LOTTERY

Design by a transcendent, rational source is, moreover, the best explanation among several for the fine-tuning of the universe.

PROFESSOR SAYS, YOU SAY

Discuss as a group what you would say if a college professor made this statement in class:

WE SHOULDN'T BE SURPRISED THAT THE UNIVERSE IS PERFECT FOR HUMAN LIFE, SINCE WE EVOLVED WITHIN THE UNIVERSE AND ITS PARAMETERS.

and/or

GIVEN THE NECESSARY NATURE OF EXISTENCE, IT'S NO SURPRISE TO DISCOVER THAT THE BASIC PARAMETERS ARE EXACTLY AS REQUIRED.

You can refer to your notes, if you took any during Dr. Meyer's lecture. Support or add to one another's responses, bringing in any relevant Bible passages. Perhaps you'd like to role-play the dialogue, taking turns to represent the professor.

WHAT OTHERS SAID

There was a young fellow from Trinity,
Who took the square root of infinity.
But the number of digits, Gave him the fidgets;
He dropped Math and took up Divinity.
  — George Gamow, *One, Two, Three ... Infinity* (1947)

WHAT IS WHAT? *A matching quiz*

Draw a line from each term in the first column to its definition in the second column.

1. **FINE-TUNING**

   A. former Cambridge physicist turned minister

2. **BIG CRUNCH**

   B. our universe is the outcome of a cosmic lottery

3. **COSMOLOGICAL CONSTANT**

   C. universe collapsing inward if its expansion rate were slower

4. **ANTHROPIC FINE-TUNING EVIDENCES**

   D. every physical parameter set just right to make the galaxies and stars possible

5. **POLKINGHORNE**

   E. fine-tuning no surprise since we wouldn't be here otherwise

6. **WEAK ANTHROPIC PRINCIPLE**

   F. vacuum energy of free space

7. **MANY WORLDS HYPOTHESIS**

   G. fine-tuned for *human* life

"The evolution of the stars and the evolving of new chemical elements in the nuclear furnaces of the stars were indispensable prerequisites for the generation of life. The laws that we understand as laws of nature had to be finely tuned to make this possible."
—John Polkinghorne

LESSON 5

DNA BY DESIGN, PART 1

— SURPRISES IN THE CELL

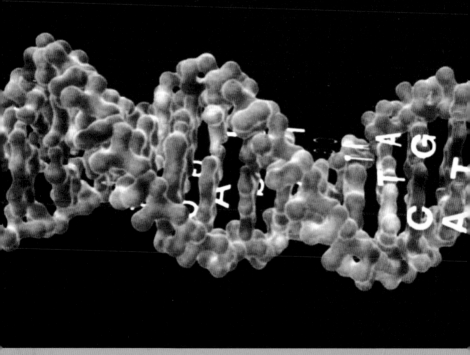

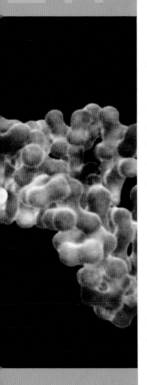

The question of design is a critical worldview-shaping paradox. If biological life looks designed, then what are we to make of it? Darwinian evolutionists believe that the scientific explanation for the appearance of design is natural selection, or "undirected causes." Simply put, they believe the design we observe is only an illusion.

However, significant evidence for intelligent design is found in the inner workings of the cell and in the complex makeup of DNA. It is becoming more and more apparent that theism provides the best explanation for the phenomena of design and information in the cells of all living things.

QUOTE UNQUOTE

What did Dr. Meyer say? Fill in the blanks as you watch his presentation.

1. New Atheism is built on this idea that there's no evidence of design in nature, that the design is an _____.

2. There's two parts of evolutionary theory—biological evolution and … _____ evolution.

3. Darwin's theory was that if you go back far enough, you get to a single, common _____.

4. Scientists soon learned that _____ were really big, long, complicated molecules.

5. Proteins are made of a string of _____ _____ that are arranged in a precise way.

6. In order for them to do their jobs, you have to have the amino acids _____ ____ in a particular way.

7. Every one of the jobs that a protein does depends on the specific _____ of that protein.

8. The arrangement of characters in the _____ is responsible for telling the cell how to construct the proteins.

9. What do we have in DNA? We have _____ information.

10. What's the fundamental mystery in life? It's the origin of _____.

WHAT'S THE BIG IDEA?

THE ORIGIN OF SPECIOUS IDEAS

Modern biology has been dominated by the Darwinist view that the appearance of intelligent design is merely an illusion caused by undirected natural selection.

An intelligent theory, huh?

So it appears.

BUT...

You can't judge a book by its content.

On the origin of species Charles Darwin

THE AMAZING CELL

Early 20th-century ideas regarding the chemical evolution of life did not account for later discoveries about the complexity of proteins and how they are formed in the cell.

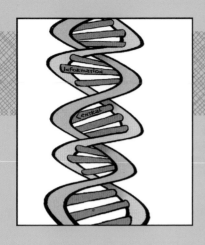

SIGNS OF A PROGRAMMER

Specified information (digital code) in the DNA molecule directs the processes within each cell, exhibiting a high degree of intelligent design.

PROFESSOR SAYS, YOU SAY

Discuss as a group what you would say if a college professor asked this question in class:

I STILL MAINTAIN THAT MANKIND "CRAWLED OUT OF THE OCEAN"! HAS SCIENCE EVER REALLY DISPROVED THAT IDEA?

You can refer to your notes, if you took any during Dr. Meyer's lecture. Support or add to one another's responses, bringing in any relevant Bible passages. Perhaps you'd like to role-play the dialogue, taking turns to represent the professor.

WHAT OTHERS SAID

"It now seems certain that the amino acid sequence of any protein is determined by the sequence of bases in some region of a particular nucleic acid molecule." —Francis Crick

"It is one of the striking generalizations of biochemistry—which surprisingly is hardly ever mentioned in the biochemical textbooks—that the 20 amino acids and the four bases, are, with minor reservations, the same throughout Nature. As far as I am aware, the presently accepted set of 20 amino acids was first drawn up by Watson and myself in the summer of 1953 in response to a letter of [George] Gamow's." —Francis Crick

"When Watson and Crick discovered the structure and information-bearing properties of DNA, they did indeed solve one mystery, namely, the secret of how the cell stores and transmits hereditary information. But they uncovered another mystery that remains with us to this day. This is the DNA enigma—the mystery of the origin of the information needed to build the first living organism." —Stephen Meyer, *Signature in the Cell*

WHAT IS WHAT? *A matching quiz*

Draw a line from each term in the first column to its definition in the second column.

1. **DAWKINS**

2. **BIOLOGICAL EVOLUTION**

3. **CHEMICAL EVOLUTION**

4. **PROTOPLASM**

5. **PREBIOTIC SOUP**

6. **SEQUENCE SPECIFICITY**

7. **CRICK**

8. **DNA**

9. **SHANNON INFORMATION**

A. how you get from simple life forms to complex

B. co-discoverer of the DNA's structure

C. how you get from chemicals to the first organism

D. proponent of New Atheism

E. imaginary ocean of amino acids at earth's beginning

F. function dependent on arrangement of the parts

G. complex data devoid of meaning

H. deoxyribonucleic acid

I. hypothetical contents of a living cell

LESSON 6

DNA BY DESIGN, PART 2

— DOING THE MATH

Odds of Getting Combination b

| 10 | sites with | 20 | amino acid |

10,000,000,000,000 possible co

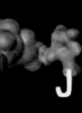

Chance

J

$= 20^{10}$

binations!!!

EW

Is it possible for life to have begun by mere chance? Where did the specified information in DNA come from? How did life first begin?

Materialistic scientists have offered several theories on how non-intelligent natural processes might explain the digital code we find in DNA. These theories include chance, natural selection, and self-organization.

However, Dr. Meyer shows the mathematical and logical difficulties that these theories face in explaining the origin of life. The conclusion is inescapable: Undirected processes do not create the information that life needs to get started.

QUOTE UNQUOTE

What did Dr. Meyer say? Fill in the blanks as you watch his presentation.

1. How many of us stop and think about the fact that the DNA molecule has digital code along the _____?

2. If you want to produce specified information, _____ alone is not a very effective mechanism.

3. In any linguistic system, the _____ possibilities are a very small, minute fraction of all the total possibilities.

4. There are _____ possible protein-forming amino acids.

5. Non-_____ bonds can't form proteins.

6. No _____ _____ thinks that life began by chance.

7. Natural selection depends upon what's called _____ reproduction.

8. Natural selection presupposes organisms that can _____ themselves.

9. What you're dealing with is a true message system, but it's not governed by _____ and _____.

10. Undirected processes do not produce the _____ you need to produce the first life.

WHAT'S THE BIG IDEA?

NOT A CHANCE!

The odds against amino acids forming a functional protein by chance are so astronomical that no serious scientist supports the chance hypothesis anymore.

Can a protein form just by chance?

I'LL WRITE DOWN THE ODDS.

Call a cab when you're done.

CART BEFORE THE HORSE

Natural selection ("necessity") cannot explain the origin of information in the first cell, since the process of selection itself requires information (DNA, proteins) that didn't exist prior to life.

Let's bake some cookies.

This recipe calls for chocolate chips and . . . cookie dough.

THE JUBILATION of Cooking

I think we have a problem.

CHEMICALS CAN'T SPELL

Molecular forces of attraction cannot explain the sequence of amino acids in the backbone of DNA.

PROFESSOR SAYS, YOU SAY

Discuss as a group what you would say if a college professor made this statement in class:

FOLKS, YOU CAN CALCULATE THE ODDS ALL YOU WANT, BUT SAYING THAT LIFE AROSE PURELY BY CHANCE STILL SEEMS LESS PREPOSTEROUS THAN CLAIMING THAT THIS WHOLE SORRY MESS WAS CREATED BY AN ETERNAL AND LOVING GOD.

You can refer to your notes, if you took any during Dr. Meyer's lecture. Support or add to one another's responses, bringing in any relevant Bible passages. Perhaps you'd like to role-play the dialogue, taking turns to represent the professor.

WHAT OTHERS SAID

"When I was in my twenties, I read James D. Watson's Molecular Biology of the Gene. . . . The understanding of life is a great subject. Biological information is the most important information we can discover." —Bill Gates, *The Road Ahead*

"The likelihood of the formation of life from inanimate matter is one to a number with 40,000 noughts after it. . . . It is big enough to bury Darwin and the whole theory of evolution. . . . If the beginnings of life were not random, they must therefore have been the product of purposeful intelligence." —Fred Hoyle

WHAT IS WHAT? *A matching quiz*

Draw a line from each term in the first column to its definition in the second column.

1. LEHNINGER

A. prebiotic natural selection

2. NECESSITY

B. originator of self-organization theory

3. SELF-ORGANIZATION

C. molecular forces of attraction create the digital code

4. KENYON

D. biochemist who advocated chance

"An intelligible communication via radio signal from some distant galaxy would be widely hailed as evidence of an intelligent source. Why then doesn't the message sequence on the DNA molecule also constitute prima facie evidence for an intelligent source? After all, DNA information is not just analogous to a message sequence such as Morse code; it is such a message sequence." —Charles B Thaxton, Walter L Bradley and Robert L Olsen, *The Mystery of Life's Origin, Reassessing Current Theories*

LESSON 7

DNA BY DESIGN, PART 3

— INFORMATION AND INTELLIGENCE

"Human DNA is like a computer but far, far more advanced than ever created."

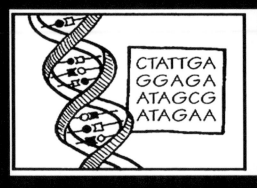

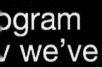

A fundamental rule of the modern scientist is that no non-naturalistic (or supernatural) concepts can be employed to explain the origin of life. Therefore, the debate regarding the origin of life is not just about the evidence itself, but also about the presuppositions that keep the scientist from considering all possible explanations.

We know that the source of any and all information found within the DNA code is intelligence itself. So where does this intelligence come from? Chance? Natural selection? Dr. Meyer has shown already that those hypotheses do not hold water. Therefore, the most plausible source of information within the universe is an intelligent designer, pointing us toward a transcendent Creator of the universe.

QUOTE UNQUOTE

What did Dr. Meyer say? Fill in the blanks as you watch his presentation.

1. If you're trying to explain an event in the remote past, you don't invoke some _____ _____, the effects of which you've never seen.

2. Whenever we trace information back to its source, invariably there's an _____.

3. Information is habitually associated with _____ activity.

4. When we find information in the DNA molecule, encoded in digital form, the most _____ conclusion is that the information had an intelligent source.

5. *The Origin of Species* is a brilliant piece of scientific reasoning. But it was based upon information that was _____.

6. _____ is necessary to explain information.

7. The _____ regions of the DNA function like an operating system within a computer.

8. Scientists say, well, maybe there was intelligent design, but that's not part of _____.

9. The fundamental obligation of the scientist is to seek out the _____ explanation.

10. The biggest and most important rule is, _____ _____ _____.

MASTER MIND

Information always comes from an intelligent source. It is associated with the conscious activity of a mind, and we know of no other cause that can produce it.

GOD DON'T MAKE JUNK

Our confidence in the New Testament's historical accuracy is based also on the evidence that the original documents were reliably transmitted to us over the centuries.

SCIENCE
WITH
BLINDERS

Modern science is driven by materialistic presuppositions, so only non-theistic explanations for the origin of life are deemed to be science.

PROFESSOR SAYS, YOU SAY

Discuss as a group what you would say if a college professor asked these questions in class:

SCIENCE STUDIES *STUFF*—WHAT WE CAN EXAMINE WITH OUR FIVE SENSES, RIGHT? SO WHY DO YOU COMPLAIN WHEN SCIENTISTS DON'T ALLOW "INTELLIGENT DESIGN" INTO THE DISCUSSION ON THE ORIGIN OF LIFE? ISN'T THAT TURNING SCIENCE INTO PHILOSOPHY OR RELIGION?

You can refer to your notes, if you took any during Dr. Meyer's lecture. Support or add to one another's responses, bringing in any relevant Bible passages. Perhaps you'd like to role-play the dialogue, taking turns to represent the professor.

WHAT OTHERS SAID

"Scientists, freely making their own choice of problems and pursuing them in the light of their own personal judgment, are in fact co-operating as members of a closely knit organization." —Michael Polanyi

"The scientific attitude implies what I call the postulate of objectivity— that is to say, the fundamental postulate that there is no plan, that there is no intention in the universe." —Jacques Monod

"According to the scientific naturalist version of cosmic history, nature is a permanently closed system of material effects that can never be influenced by something from outside—like God, for example." —Phillip Johnson

"In short, the proposition that God was in any way involved in our creation is effectively outlawed, and implicitly negated." —Phillip Johnson

WHAT IS WHAT? *A matching quiz*

Draw a line from each term in the first column to its definition in the second column.

1. *EXPELLED*

2. LYELL

3. SIGNATURE IN THE CELL

4. "JUNK DNA"

5. ENCODE PROJECT

6. METHODOLOGICAL NATURALISM

A. Dr. Meyer's book on DNA

B. Darwin's mentor

C. DNA sections that do not direct the building of proteins

D. search for functions performed by noncoding DNA

E. documentary film hosted by Ben Stein

F. only materialistic theories allowed

"If we've defined science such that it cannot get to the true answer, we've got a pretty lame definition of science." —Douglas Axe

"If the universe is the product of blind, mechanistic forces, how do we know it has any intelligible structure at all?... Where is the guarantee that the concepts in our minds bear any relation to the world outside?" —Nancy R. Pearcey and Charles B. Thaxton, *The Soul of Science*

LESSON 8

THE RETURN OF THE GOD HYPOTHESIS

The Cambrian Explosion

present ——————————————————————

younger rocks

530-525 mya

- 200 mya
- 400 mya
- 600 mya
- 800 mya

older rocks

08 OVERV

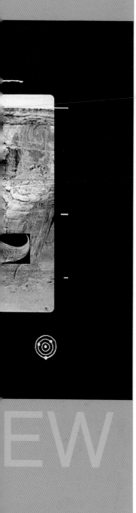

"He has caused his wonders to be remembered."

— *Psalm 111:4, NIV*

Let's stop and review. When one takes all the evidence into account, from the finite beginning and fine-tuning of the universe, to the digital information and operating system in the living cell, there is a compelling case to be made for the existence of God. In fact, it may be the only intelligent theory left standing—the best plausible explanation for the origin of the universe and life itself.

EW

QUOTE UNQUOTE

What did Dr. Meyer say? Fill in the blanks as you watch his presentation.

1. If you have a different _____, you can come in for some pretty severe ridicule.

2. I was studying a subject that had been shaped by people who _____ _____ _____.

3. Science is a fantastic tool for studying the _____ _____ _____ _____.

4. If you go back far enough in time, the universe _____ infinitely tightly, so that it had a zero point in space.

5. From the very beginning of the universe, the laws of physics and chemistry were very _____ _____.

6. We looked at the evidence from cosmology and physics and saw that there was evidence for an intelligent and _____ cause.

7. We're talking about machine code—_____ in the cell.

8. We live in the generation when many of God's _____ that were long hidden are being revealed.

9. If you want to explain the origin of life, you have to first explain the origin of the _____ that would be needed to produce the first life.

10. There's evidence of design at _____ intervals further along the biological timeline.

WONDERS TO BE REMEMBERED

Theism—with its affirmation of a transcendent, powerful, and intelligent Creator—provides the best explanation of the key evidences concerning the origin of the universe and life.

MAMMALS OUT OF NOWHERE

The fossil record shows the sudden appearance of new life forms at discrete intervals throughout history.

REPENTANT SCIENTISTS

Whether in cosmology, physics, or biology, modern science has recently gathered so much evidence for intelligent design that some scientists are returning to the age-old belief that God is behind it all.

PROFESSOR SAYS, YOU SAY

Discuss as a group what you would say if a college professor launched into this rant:

I AM A SCIENTIST ... A *SCIENTIST!* SO EVEN THOUGH I AM PUZZLED AND CHALLENGED BY THE APPEARANCE OF DESIGN THROUGHOUT NATURE, HOW COULD I EVER ACCEPT THE NOTION THAT THIS CREATOR OF YOURS BECAME ONE OF US? AND SO ON ... HE VISITED THE EARTH, DIED, AND SPRANG TO LIFE AGAIN! THIS IS THE STUFF OF FAIRY TALES.

You can refer to your notes, if you took any during Dr. Meyer's lecture. Support or add to one another's responses, bringing in any relevant Bible passages. Perhaps you'd like to role-play the dialogue, taking turns to represent the professor.

WHAT OTHERS SAID

"Such indeed is the respect paid to science, that the most absurd opinions may become current, provided they are expressed in language, the sound of which recalls some well-known scientific phrase." —James Clerk Maxwell, 1871

"The notion that ... the operating program of a living cell could be arrived at by chance in a primordial soup here on earth is evidently nonsense of a high order." —Fred Hoyle

"Suspicions about Darwin's theory arise for two reasons. The first: the theory makes no sense. The second: it is supported by little evidence." —David Berlinski

WHAT IS WHAT? *A matching quiz*

Draw a line from each term in the first column to its definition in the second column.

1. **MAXWELL**

2. **HUBBLE**

3. **WATSON AND CRICK**

4. **MATERIALISM**

5. **DEISM**

6. **CAMBRIAN EXPLOSION**

7. **BIG BLOOM**

8. *DARWIN'S BLACK BOX*

9. **FLEW**

A. discovered DNA structure

B. "irreducibly complex" machinery in the cell

C. one of the three greatest physicists of all time

D. discovered the expanding universe

E. sudden appearance of flowering plants

F. God created and then abandoned the world

G. atheism

H. philosopher who gave up atheism

I. sudden appearance of major forms of life

"The theory of evolution ... will be one of the great jokes in the history books of the future. Posterity will marvel that so flimsy and dubious an hypothesis could be accepted with the incredible credulity it has."
—Malcolm Muggeridge

EW

It is impossible to live as a moral relativist. Most people acknowledge some standard of right and wrong, but what is that standard and where did it come from? In this lesson, Dr. Meyer moves away from science and cosmology to discuss the philosophical and ethical arguments for the existence of God.

QUOTE UNQUOTE

What did Dr. Meyer say? Fill in the blanks as you watch his presentation.

1. Only if you believe in God can you give a sensible account of what it means for something to be _____ and _____.

2. God is a necessary condition of there being an _____ morality.

3. If God is dead, then all things are _____.

4. In pantheism, the distinction between you and me is _____.

5. Materialists believe that ethics are purely relative; they are merely personal _____.

6. If you're going to say somebody _____ to have done something, that presupposes that the person could have made the choice to do so.

7. It's impossible to live with the philosophy of moral _____.

8. To have a system of objective morals, we really need to have a reason to regard humans as _____.

9. The idea of _____ derived from the idea that there was an intrinsic dignity for each person.

10. From a Darwinian point of view, there is no qualitative difference between humans and _____.

WHAT GOD WROTE ON OUR HEARTS

All people have an inborn sense of right and wrong, and this can be explained only by the existence of God (theism).

FAITHS THAT DON'T FIT THE FACTS

No other worldview is consistent with our possessing an objective moral code.

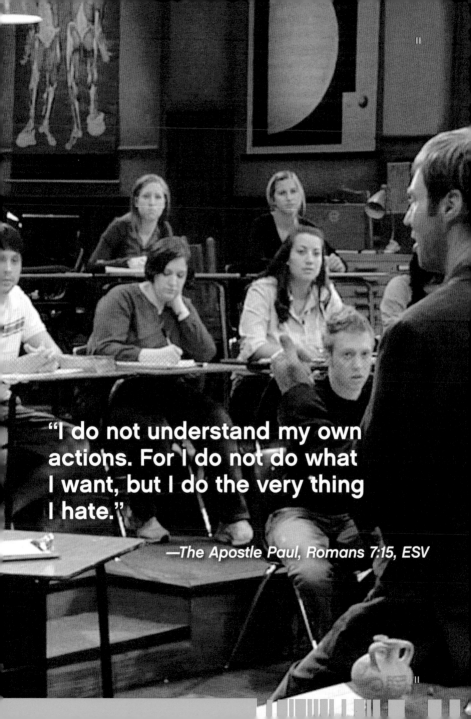

"I do not understand my own actions. For I do not do what I want, but I do the very thing I hate."

—*The Apostle Paul, Romans 7:15, ESV*

PROFESSOR SAYS, YOU SAY

Discuss as a group what you would say if a college professor made this statement in class:

YOU SEEM INTOLERANT OF PEOPLE WHO ADVOCATE THE "IF IT FEELS GOOD, DO IT" APPROACH TO SEX. BUT PEOPLE ARE WHO THEY ARE; THEY'RE JUST GOING TO DO WHAT COMES NATURALLY. SO TO ATTACK SUCH DIVERSE BEHAVIOR IS WRONG.

You can refer to your notes, if you took any during Dr. Meyer's lecture. Support or add to one another's responses, bringing in any relevant Bible passages. Perhaps you'd like to role-play the dialogue, taking turns to represent the professor.

WHAT OTHERS SAID

"A sinister current of influence ran from Darwin's theory of evolution to Hitler's policy of extermination." —David Berlinski

"Whenever you find a man who says he does not believe in a real Right and Wrong, you will find the same man going back on this a moment later. He may break his promise to you, but if you try breaking one to him he will be complaining 'It's not fair' before you can say Jack Robinson." —C.S. Lewis, *Mere Christianity*

"The most important human endeavor is the striving for morality in our actions. Our inner balance and even our very existence depend on it. Only morality in our actions can give beauty and dignity to life." —Charles Dickens

"When legitimacy yields to force, and moral absolutes to relativism, a great darkness descends and angels become indistinguishable from devils." —Paul Johnson, *Modern Times*

WHAT IS WHAT? *A matching quiz*

Draw a line from each term in the first column to its definition in the second column.

1. **VIRTUE ETHICS**

2. **DUALISM**

3. **RELATIVISM**

4. **SCOPES**

5. **LEOPOLD AND LOEB**

6. **DIMINISHED RESPONSIBILITY**

7. **KINSEY REPORTS**

8. **PETER SINGER**

9. *MEIN KAMPF*

A. distinction

B. Hitler's plea for survival of the fittest race

C. morality stems from God's character and how He designed human beings

D. 1920 trial against biology teacher advocating evolution

E. no objective or higher standard

F. if it feels good sexually, do it

G. a baby is worth less than a pig or dog

H. college students who killed for the thrill of it

I. innocent by virtue of impaired thinking

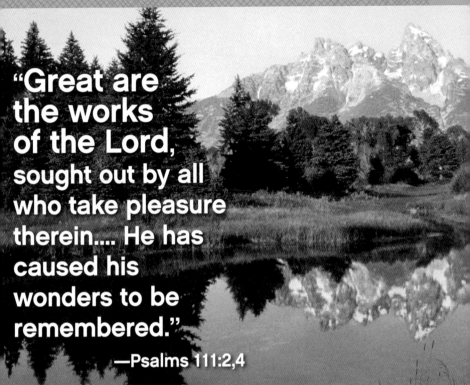

"Great are the works of the Lord, sought out by all who take pleasure therein.... He has caused his wonders to be remembered."

—Psalms 111:2,4

© PhotoDisc

In this capstone lesson, Dr. Meyer explains why neither relativism nor evolutionary ethics can provide the basis for a coherent understanding of right and wrong. By studying the actions of all human beings, we see that everyone points to an objective moral code, and the most likely source of that code is a transcendent standard.

With that we conclude our survey of evidence for the existence of God. After studying the cosmos, the cell, and human behavior, we are filled with confidence not only that God is real, but also that He has left evidence of Himself we can share with others.

EW

QUOTE UNQUOTE

What did Dr. Meyer say? Fill in the blanks as you watch his presentation.

1. If you're going to say "_____," you have to be able to give me a basis for that.

2. We're not _____ in other realms of life, but for some reason we think it's a justified position when we're talking about moral reality.

3. It doesn't actually follow that just because people make different ethical judgments, they have different _____ _____.

4. You say the tuna salad is rotten; I say it's great. Does that mean that there is nothing _____ about the tuna salad?

5. The relativist has to say, well it looks like they're having an argument about right and wrong, but all they're really arguing about is _____.

6. If relativism is true, it implies there can be no ethical _____.

7. Relativism implies that _____ in ethics is impossible.

8. As soon as you realize what morality is from the evolutionary point of view, you have no real reason to _____ it.

9. How do you give an account of "_____" when it all comes from the same source, an impersonal evolutionary mechanism?

10. We have evidence both from science and from philosophy (or ethics) that suggests that belief in God provides a _____ explanatory framework for all of experience.

THE WRECKAGE OF RELATIVISM

Relativism fails to provide a coherent explanation of our moral experience. We were not made to live that way.

Can I cheat on the exam?

I can't say it's wrong, but it's not my preference.

GOING AGAINST OUR GENES

Evolutionary ethics cannot provide a coherent explanation of our moral experience.

REASONS TO BELIEVE

When your faith in God is based on scientific evidence and moral reasoning rather than feelings alone, then you will be able to confidently step up and contend for God's truth in the public arena.

Discuss as a group what you would say if a college professor made this statement in class:

WE'VE ARGUED OVER DESIGN IN NATURE, AND WE'VE DEBATED THE EXISTENCE OF AN OBJECTIVE MORAL CODE. I RESPECT YOUR TENACITY, AND I THINK YOU ARE ENTITLED TO BELIEVE WHAT YOU WISH. BUT WHAT I DON'T UNDERSTAND IS WHY YOU WANT OTHERS TO BELIEVE IT TOO. WHY NOT JUST LEAVE EVERYONE TO FIND HIS OR HER OWN TRUTH?

You can refer to your notes, if you took any during Dr. Meyer's lecture. Support or add to one another's responses, bringing in any relevant Bible passages. Perhaps you'd like to role-play the dialogue, taking turns to represent the professor.

WHAT OTHERS SAID

"You probably want to be safe much more than you want to help the man who is drowning: but the Moral Law tells you to help him all the same. And surely it often tells us to try to make the right impulse stronger than it naturally is?" —C.S. Lewis, *Mere Christianity*

"Overwhelming strong proofs of intelligent and benevolent design lie around us.... The atheistic idea is so nonsensical that I cannot put it into words." —Lord Kelvin

"In your hearts honor Christ the Lord as holy, always being prepared to make a defense to anyone who asks you for a reason for the hope that is in you." 1 Peter 3:15, ESV